SIXTY!

CELEBRATING DIAMOND YEARS OF
MINISTRY AND MARRIAGE

with

Poetry and Reflections

from

Patricia Batstone

This Collection © Patricia Batstone 2025

All rights reserved. No part of this publication may be reproduced, stored in a retrieval system, or transmitted in any form or by any means, electronic, mechanical, photocopying, recording or otherwise, without the prior written permission of the Author.

There is, however, no restriction on verbal presentation. Copyright must be attributed at all times.

British Library Cataloguing in Publication Data.

A catalogue record for this book is available from the British Library

ISBN 978 0 86071 952 6

Photographs:

Front Cover – *17th July 1965*

Back cover – *Christmas Day 2024*

Published on behalf of the Author by
MOORLEYS
Print, Design & Publishing
info@moorleys.co.uk · www.moorleys.co.uk

The views, thoughts, and opinions expressed in this book belong solely to the author, and do not necessarily reflect the views of Moorleys Print & Publishing Ltd or any of its associates

CONTENTS

Page

INTRODUCTION 1

In Perpetuum 2

TIMES AND SEASONS
Seasonal Shifts 3
One Flame 4
Twenty-Twelve 4
Lamb in Winter 5
Seed of Life 6
Winter Ice 7
Earth is Our Gift 8
Leaf 9
War Zone 10
Rain 11
Fifteenth July 2019 12
Summer is for Living – *Davidian* 13
September Song 13
Maundy Thursday 2021 14
The Face of Love 15
No Room 16
Eighty Today! 18
Trinity Twenty-One 19
Remembrance 2021 19

PEOPLE AND PLACES
To Nancy – At Her Century 20
To Blanche 21
Birthday Villanelle 22
The Qualities of Love 23
Sylvia Remembered 24
I Will Wear Purple 25
The Ballad of John Bunyan 26
Abraham: An Iffy Kind of Faith 29
Moses 30

No Waiting 31
I Am the Man 32
Journey's End..33
Wish You Were Here!...35
Watching People Watching People Watching
    the Grand Canyon 36
The Village...37
Divine Experiment – *Tetrachtys* 40
Damp in Devon 41
Coming Back to St. Olave's 42
Soft Shoes 43
Specification – *Haiku*...43
Wales is Another Country......................................44
Desire - *Davidian* 45

POETRY AND PRAYER
Old Poems 46
Just a Chip..47
Sun, Sea, Sand 48
Competition..49
Pages in God's Story 50
The Ballad of a 'Lost' Sheep....................................51
Summer Haiku 51
Without the Blueprint 52
Multiplication Table – *Haiku*...................................52
A Modern Masterpiece..53
Silent Painting 54
Promise – *Haiku*..54
The Only Decent Miracle 55
Music of Life 55
A Century of Song..56
God's Music..57
God of All Gifts 58
Just a Perfect Number 59
Don't Switch Off!..60
Defining Love 61
Shepherding 62
Raised to Heights Sublime 63

MINISTRY AND MISSION
    The Arrival 64
    This One Moment 65
    Speaking His Name 66
    An Alternative Creed 67
    Impossible Tasks 69
    Creative Therapy: Facing the Question -
        in Search of an Answer 70
    A Rare Thing 72
    For Many Generations 73
    Connect 74
    The Modern Babel 75
    Knowing God 75
    Listen! 76
    Deep in The Heart 77
    Too Busy to Listen 78
    Prayer Seventy-Five 80
    Remembrance 81
    Twilight Hope 82

Acknowledgments 83

Publications in Print 84

POETRY FORMS

Haiku – three lines of 7–5–7 syllables.

Davidian – A form devised by poet Wendy Webb of five line stanzas of 10-10-10-10-6 syllables;
OR reverse Davidian – 6-10-10-10-10 syllables.

Tetrachtys – Ten lines of 1–2–3–4–10 syllables, reversed to 10-4-3-2-1.

INTRODUCTION

In 2021, I compiled a selection of eighty poems and reflections to celebrate our eightieth birthdays. The years 2024/25 highlight two other milestones – December 2024 marked sixty years from my accreditation as a Methodist Local Preacher and July 2025 celebrates our Diamond Wedding. So with those events in mind, another book seemed appropriate, although limiting the hundreds of unpublished pieces to around sixty proved impossible.

With the exception of special events necessarily following one another, they are not presented in chronological order; rather in an appropriate order for their subject-matter. Inevitably, some subjects will be prominent in all categories – Biblical references, for instance, or particular times in life; equally, the present prominence of the state of the natural world cannot long be ignored.

So they are divided into four sections. Firstly, **Times and Seasons** – not the four natural seasons only but the church's seasons, major events in the calendar, personal events, and, because of its impact, some of the thoughts engendered by the 'Covid season'.

Then there are **People and Places** – not only those we know personally but, given my role as a preacher, inevitably people in the Bible and history I'd written about, together with places visited or special for some reason. These two areas fall into defined sub-sections.

Poetry and Prayers are food and drink for me and much behind that and other gifts is included. Prayers tend to be those focusing on creativity and especially the Giver of all gifts. The aim is less to be preachy than perhaps provocative, challenging, even inspirational.

Finally, **Ministry and Mission**, which look out on to the more practical side of being Christians and of our relationships with community and the wider world. Ministry essentially begins with the personal call and then moves outward to mission within the community and the wider world. In fact, environmental concerns are never far from any section.

By and large I have resisted including verses written for personal celebrations – some are for another time and place and special just to us, while others have already been included in other publications, so are not repeated here. These are my gifts to those who appreciate poetry of any kind, with my prayer that they will both speak to you and through you to others.

Patricia Batstone

IN PERPETUUM

*Every day is a new beginning.
Every night an ending
carried forward.*

[January 2022]

TIMES AND SEASONS

SEASONAL SHIFTS

Times and seasons, how they come and go:
January's icy hand presages spring;
February leaps for days in short supply;
March brings winds to rage and huff and blow.

April's golden Easter glows with Grace;
May is shining white at Pentecost.
June's brief summer blushes as a bride,
July's scorching sting is death too soon.

August is the month of sea and sand,
September is harvested in gold.
October colours, blazing amber,
November lighting fires on the fifth.

Last, December, Advent hope renewed –
Times and seasons, how they come and go.

December 2007

ONE FLAME

Advent candle –
floating in a pristine world of clear cut glass,
single flame
lighting up the window,
casting shadows on my hand.
Illuminating
light reflected on the glass
like stars dancing in the atmosphere,
spreading rays to every vacant space.

One flame,
flame to mark beginning,
flame of promise for today and all week long:
I am one of God's people, frail and irresponsible
yet counted in
to share the promised coming
of my Lord.

December 2001

TWENTY-TWELVE

This year of celebration
has caught imagination.
Looking back, looking on,
run the race till it is done –
but may this day for you alone
bring blessings more than you have known,
with joy and happiness and strength
to run the race and win at length.

LAMB IN WINTER

Stark by the broken fencing,
feet sunk in winter snow,
you turn your back on history
and ponder a closed gate.

White wool against the muddied field,
little black face turned upward,
away from the trees and sky,
contemplating survival.

Trapped by alien elements,
stick legs black like match heads
rising out of the deep snow sea,
looking away, you see nothing.

Little lamb grown old, waiting,
your body redolent with unborn life
seeking home and shelter
you miss the guiding star.

Dear Sheep, the Shepherd comes,
though distant, out of view,
to carry you, your precious load, and his,
safely through the gate.

December 2000 - Inspired by an illustration on an Abbey Pottery jug.

SEED OF LIFE

I am a seed being planted in the uninviting autumn earth
that turns too soon to winter ice.
In its white snow covering that squeezes through to reach me,
I lie, shivering, gasping for each faint drip
to moisten some small space. I need some warmth:
the watery sun sends lukewarm softening rays.

Time passes. A sudden burst of energy and now
I am not cold and dry but damp with dew and growing faintly warm.
Two green shoots are bursting from my head – the pain! –
and down below I feel the earth with spindly roots I struggle to project.
Achievement gives me life, and food: no longer empty
I am being fed from warm brown earth, and I can rest.

Each day becomes less stressful.
My shoots have pushed their way towards the sun, and now
the sense of freedom is immense.
Too soon the change as I am blown and battered by the winds.
No longer free, but bound to earth in wind and rain
that beat their own discordant harmony against my will.

I open up again, to silence, and the dampening rain-soaked air.
I stretch my stem and quickly find new strength. I am alive!
My bud will soon become a flower,
I straighten up, to push the bud a little way,
and see the faint pink blossom hunched beneath.
Another day will bring that bloom to birth.

Now I have youth and beauty at my head,
but such frail loveliness lives for so short a time.
As petals start unfolding I need dew for sustenance
as bees need me and burrow at my heart.

Spring turns to summer, warms me, helps me flourish,
be a pleasure to all who see and care, till autumn looms.
I am older now, my beautiful pink petals tinged with rust
begin to fall and sink into the muddy earth
under a leafy covering arranged by whispering wind.

My short span runs, lulled by heat, disturbed by wind and
soon the frost
that kills the shoots, and hardens earth again around my
roots.
Then as they die so I shall die, for rootless there's no life in me
–
except one tiny seed from that pink flower
should fall to earth and, nurtured, rise again, new-grown.

                                                    2003

WINTER ICE

    Ice, shining in the half-light,
    the detritus of human carelessness
    stunned, the weir
    petrified in flow.
    Vandals search for stones to dim the sheen
    and shatter the eerie stillness.
    They fail.
    I trudge on into the damp darkness,
    over the bridge, weary for home.

                                           December 1996

EARTH IS OUR GIFT

Earth is our gift – how we have squandered it! –
polluted the atmosphere,
drained off the moisture,
dried up the river-beds,
cut down the forests,
poisoned the soil,
transmitted diseases,
rotted the leaves
that waved in the breeze;
looted the gold-mines,
stolen the jewels,
melted the ice-caps,
uprooted the trees;
left wild the garden
planted with love,
then to their devices
wild-growing weeds.

Given the gift – the best God created,
we have abused, misused
and spent all the beauty.
Now we are penitents, seeking to halt
the spread of disaster, all of our fault.
May He in His mercy
see how we repent
and teach us anew
what a treasure we've spent.

Now each new-born spring
may we find the assurance
that we are forgiven,
the dance
still in motion
till time is no more.

October 2002 - Based on Genesis 2:4b-15

LEAF

Fallen leaf,
contemplated,
hard veins,
damp, dying edges,
brown
in autumn decay.
Leaves under water,
sunk into the mass;
one leaf
contemplated,
taken, drawn,
discarded
yet preserved
indefinitely,
its transient beauty
caught before decay –
the beauty of beholding
held on camera
for posterity –
leaves and ashes
scattered to the wind.

August 2002 – Written at the Thelma Hulbert Gallery, Honiton based on a scene from a 'Temp' video showing artist Thelma Hulbert taking a leaf from a fountain and later painting it.

WAR ZONE

The attack was swift and unexpected.
Even as she sat, innocent of any crime,
contemplating the weeks of gestation, days now,
the enemy struck from above – or was it behind?
She couldn't fathom – if didn't even matter.
She escaped as her home fell about her,
her unborn family lurching under the pressure,
cracked and bruised.

Safe under the evergreen she watched in disbelief
as the enemy knelt to add his tears to her own,
scooped up the shattered fragments of her home,
restored, rebuilt, and left for her design.
Her loss was no one's gain –
      one past redeeming,
        two who might be saved.
Dare she take risks for life?
Her very nature told her No,
and yet ...?

Silent now,
the night grew dark and cold.

♥

April 2003 - Written on hearing that my husband had accidentally tipped a robin and her eggs out of its garden flower pot nest. Against all hope, she did not return to it.

RAIN

Rain, rain, rain.
They wanted it, these gardeners
but while they bask in bliss
and watch the knife-throws splashing on the ground
the rest of us get wet.
Even jumping one small space
was just too much for comfort.

Rain, rain, rain.
Symbol of depression to the lonely
who stare from empty windows
out on to the bleak streets
without belonging to the few bedraggled children
rushing home to tea.

Rain, rain, rain.
Thunder on the roofs, pouring from the gullies,
washing life away,
throwing up the floods,
transforming concrete into paddling pools
and rivers into seas of wantonness.

Rain. Rain. Rain.
The angry tears of heaven pouring to earth's heart
to drown its sorrows, wash away its guilt,
baptise its spirit to submissiveness.
Then it will rise, refreshed, redeemed,
accept its fate, prick out its loneliness
and shine its sun upon a better place.

October 2003

FIFTEENTH JULY 2019

It didn't rain!
Saint Swithun's sun burst bright
and all seemed well –
at least within my view,
if not within myself
or so much of the world
where either rains don't come
or never stop.

But could it keep it up for forty days?
The forecasters said not
and gave it four!
And yet it was **his** day.
They'd long ago committed him
to his eternal rest
and knowledge has replaced his influence
and all the superstition in his name.

Does he now rest in peace
his anger swallowed up in ecstasy?
Too many years have gone
to hold such grudge
and those who flouted wishes long away.
Has he now realised how well they meant
to honour him, not disobey?

Humility can go too far beyond the grave –
much better tell the world of his example,
laud him and give encouragement
for generations yet unborn to follow on,
embrace his humble spirit in **their** lives
till rain and shine alike
illuminate the world
with that same love of God
that shone from Swithun's life
and gave him sanctity.

SUMMER IS FOR LIVING

Summer is for living, not for lazing,
the sun's warm rays now soothe away the stress
and bringing out the best, so every song
bursts in to make the conqueror ever strong
and close the gates of wonder.

2001 - Davidian

SEPTEMBER SONG

September colours.
Sun gold Van Gogh's sunflowers,
mirroring his chair,
grey legs stark in the softness.
A song rises,
hallowing the sun,
quickening with a dancing pace,
gleaming golden top, spinning,
music merging with the colours –
September colours,
gold, straw, cream –
a shining, dancing, sunflower song.

September 2001 – Written during a Poetry Workshop led by poet Doris Corti of the Society of Women Writers and Journalists at Nutford House, London.

The Covid Season...

MAUNDY THURSDAY 2021

And it began ...

First there was the supper –
    the meal we cannot join this year.
He washed their feet,
master became their servant –
    no foot-washing ceremonies now to embarrass
    - or recall.
He gave them bread and wine –
his body and his blood –
    Such communion is banned today.
He knew who was his enemy,
the man who'd sold his life –
    He has those enemies today.

And out into the garden
he led his weary friends -
    a garden space is all we have just now.
He knew his time to die was almost here
and prayed it might not come.
    Today death strikes so randomly
    that none are free to live.

And while he knelt in agony upon a rock
his tired disciples slept the time away.
He woke them once – twice – thrice –
pleading for their company.
They let him down.
    This year we will fail him too.

And so the moment came when freedom fled
and rough hands held him fast;
when too his friends deserted him
or thought to wield a sword in his defence.
"That's not the way," he said,
healing his captor as he spoke,
turning then away from fear and willingly
walking to his death.
    Today we have our other fears –
    disease and death still stalk the world
    and leave us questioning
    our right to live.

♥

THE FACE OF LOVE

Lord God, you command us to love –
not the fluffy romantic human love,
the word flipped off the tongue without meaning –
but real, deep-down and energising love –
a love that first loves you because you love,
a love that seeds and flourishes
in loving those who need you most,
in whom I see your face –
the Face of all-embracing Love.

December 2021

NO ROOM...

... there was no room for them at the inn. [Luke 2:7b]

"Sorry, but we're fully booked."
No room for just one more
wanting to raise a Hallelujah
on this Easter Day.

There was no room for Jesus once.
The inn was full to bursting point –
but space was found for Mary
giving birth.

Sometimes there was no room for those
who hung on every word he spoke –
but wily Zacchaeus found his view
high up in a sycamore -

but not concealed from one,
for Jesus knew him, called him down,
sought a welcome in his space –
and Zacchaeus made him room.

And when he'd died so publicly
a pain-filled death on cruel cross
one found him room to lay in dignity
not knowing time would be so short.

But now, on this his Resurrection Day
the doors are barred and bolted fast
preserving space a-plenty
to keep his loved-ones out.

And where the doors have stayed ajar
there's space between the social-distanced few
who are invited in (appointment only)
to celebrate in silence, thoughtfully.

Meanwhile in city street, by urban ponds,
or in the parks and gardens of our towns
in legal limit numbers pilgrims meet
to recollect another garden scene.

And all alone in houses, flats, small rooms
lonely people long for fellowship,
desperate to communicate
with flesh and blood, not foggy screens.

What price the memories we hold
of early vigils under rising sun
when we could celebrate the Easter dawn
and sing our hymns as birds began **their** song?

And then together breakfasting,
extending fellowship and fun,
then down the hill to churches' open doors
and sanctuaries bedecked in daffodils,

where we could worship, share communion,
sing our resurrection hymns
and go out freely back into the world
to chocolate eggs and every Easter treat.

If we had known what coming years would bring,
when stripped of every opportunity
to love and laugh and sing our homilies
would we have cherished those times more?

Now as the sun streams through the panes
of too-familiar windows in our homes,
we hope and pray and wonder when the day
will come when we can love and live again
more socially.

EIGHTY TODAY!

I ought to write a verse to celebrate
    or self-commiserate
    advancing years –
    another decade looms
    uncertainly –

except, the muse reflects the way I feel –
    ageing, aching,
    wallowing self-pitily
    amidst a sea of flowers,
    blooming on knife-edges,
    dying irretrievably.

I see in them a pattern of my days,
    some wilting,
    some resurgent
    touching life –
    happy interludes
    within the pain
    of growing old.

♥

July 2021 - celebrating within the numerical parameters of social distancing.

TRINITY TWENTY-ONE

God,
  Loving, caring, healing God –
  bless me now.

Jesus,
  Saving, giving, faithful Lord –
  guide me now.

Spirit
  Infusing, enabling, powerful force –
  fill me now.

  Holy Lord, One in Three, Three in One,
  Mysterious, ever-present,
  come closer now.

May 2021

❁ ✿ ❁ ✿ ❁

REMEMBRANCE 2021

Silent the poppies fall
red raindrops on still heads
remembering death,
praying for peace.

November 2021 - No participation in Remembrance Day in 2021 – only the remembrance of the television broadcast from the Albert Hall.

Sixty

PEOPLE AND PLACES

People...

TO NANCY – AT HER CENTURY

This century has seen so many changes –
  speed, flight,
  moving images, and light
  at fingertips:
  wonderful inventions, power-driven,
  feats undreamed of on the day
  that you were born.

What hasn't changed? What quality of life
has borne you down the years
and made you who you are –
one gentle, loving soul
who meted out encouragement
and made this humble poet gain her wings
and fly to realms unknown, unthought before?

You have not changed, except to grow more gracious:
even through the weaknesses and loss
when others grieved for you,
your care was still to those not seen
but thought of always through the tears.
Faces may weather, memory lose its way
and yet we still may welcome you this day,
inhabiter of minds and hearts,
loving and beloved, and held by Love
beyond our understanding.

Age brings its wisdom, cements faith, epitomises hope
when all is founded on the solid Rock of God.
Today we thank Him as we celebrate -
a hundred years of caring – just for you.
Add my thanks to all the messages today
for giving me a corner in your heart –
and though so far away, remember this:
there'll always be a space for you in mine.

May 1999 – For Nancy Taylor, a dear friend, on the occasion of her hundredth birthday. We met Nancy at our first visit to the Methodist School of Fellowship holiday in 1977 and we remained firm friends thereafter. Nancy died in January 2000.

TO BLANCHE

Take time, and rest awhile.
Live on memories:
rejoice in youth, maturity,
reflect on love,
set sadness in its place
and see these ninety years
as steps toward a great event,
a celebration not of age
but fellowship,
the never-being-aloneness
of having as a Friend
the One who journeys with you
everywhere.

October 1999 - Blanche was a friend from Honiton Methodist Church.

BIRTHDAY VILLANELLE

To My Grandson

I send you greetings for this special date
that says you have been with us just one year –
an event we want the world to celebrate.

With smiles and looks you aim to captivate
and winning ways to bring a lot of cheer –
I send you greetings for this special date.

It is a day when we congratulate
your progress through a year oft' hard to bear –
an event we want the world to celebrate.

And soon you'll stand, walk tall and contemplate
a view made brighter by your presence there.
I send you greetings for this special date.

And one day, too, you will communicate -
then think of all the wonders we will share:
an event we want the world to celebrate.

Too soon the years will pass – two, four, six, eight –
and you will be a man: meanwhile, this year
I send you greetings for this special date,
an event we want the world to celebrate.

For James Benjamin Batstone – written for 1st November 1998.

THE QUALITIES OF LOVE

Love is patient –
    watching, quietly
    in the shadows,
    waiting opportunities
    to be.

Love is courageous
    overcoming barriers,
    defeating all things
    standing in the way,
    intent on being
    what it is.

Love is silent
    when anger looms,
    willing peace,
    comfortingly
    when the moment comes
    to be.

Love is All
    we want or need
    to go through life
    in harmony -
    then it is free
    to be.

Written October 2023 for the wedding of Noel and Virginija Batstone, 10th February 2024.

SYLVIA REMEMBERED

11th February 1988

How many bitter hours did you spend musing where I sit now?
And were these same pigeons that crowd my feet your companions then?
There was no lone pilgrim mourning you in life
But now he comes, and others will,
Remembering.

He sits alone, in thought, and contemplates the words you wrote –
Your final chapters in a dialogue with death; we capture memories and share
Opinions. He takes one final photo, sadly turns to go,
Feels cheated of your last grim lines,
Remembering.

I walk the streets you must have walked a hundred times,
But my first glimpse is of a glorious sun-bathed day
While your last hours in the beloved Poet's house, brief paradise
Speak magic worn away beyond the mercy of
Remembering.

Written on 25th anniversary of the death of Sylvia Plath, in Regent's Park and Parliament Fields Hills, London. She had died at 23 Fitzroy Road, former home of poet W. H. Auden.

I WILL WEAR PURPLE

Today I will wear purple –
purple for passion, palm and cross,
purple, the colour of kings,
of majesty,
of Lent;
purple for mourning, for tears,
for Good Friday veils.
I will wear purple today –
to fix my mind
to think of death.
    But not all day –
    only enough to show
    that I am one with suffering;
    and yet I shall not fast or weep,
    just wear purple, symbolically.

And tomorrow?
Tomorrow, purple cast aside,
I shall wear gold, the gold of hope –
the gold of daffodils, of marigolds,
of rod, cascading corn –
the gold of queens, of jewelled bands
that token knots invisibly –
the dazzling gold of love
in resurrection hue.
    Yes, tomorrow
    and tomorrow
    and tomorrows as they rise
    I'll wear the shining gold and live
    with hope, and faith, in Love.

March 2005 – Remembering Beryl, whose father would not permit her to wear purple!

THE BALLAD OF JOHN BUNYAN

John Bunyan was a tinker
  who roved the world abroad,
with pots and pans for selling
  to those who could afford

to pay the kind of prices
  designed to con the rich
while the poor, like he, went begging
  to buy a meagre stitch.

John Bunyan was a drinker,
  a man both crude and coarse,
sang bawdy songs, with language
  that made him very hoarse.

When sober he was gentle,
  a loving family man,
but drinking changed his character;
  out of control he ran,

and shouting very loudly
  with blasphemies galore
he offended all who heard him
  till they could take no more.

One day he went to mattins
  and heard the Sabbath Law,
but afterwards on village green,
  he broke it all the more –

until a voice came down from heaven
  upon his parlous state:
"John Bunyan, will you go to hell
  or heaven? Now seal your fate."

Cut to the quick he set his mind
    to mending all his ways,
amazing all who knew him
    and eliciting their praise.

But pride goes full before a fall
    and suddenly he knew
that faith abounded not in works
    but in conviction true.

His chains fell off, he sallied forth,
    a sinner, saved by grace;
no longer seeking worldly sport
    but sight of Saviour's face.

And all his customers were told
    the Gospel, fair and square:
salvation was his watchword,
    of danger he'd no care.

He ended up in prison,
    cold, wet in Bedford gaol,
but rejoicing in the Spirit
    not drowning him in ale.

John Bunyan was a thinker
    and while confined and lone,
he wrote of his conversion,
    his lifestyle to atone.

And too, he was a dreamer,
    and through long nights he saw
the path to God wide open
    as never known before.

So he became a writer –
    words flew across the page –
and the story of John Bunyan
    confronts the present age.

It holds out hope of glory,
    and challenges each soul
who reaches from a life of sin
    towards a heavenly goal.

John Bunyan was a preacher
    who had the gift of words,
despite so little schooling
    he lived to see rewards.

He was a Nonconformist
    in days when it spelled death,
and from the day he met his Lord
    until with dying breath

he sought the best for everyone
    who'd raucously denied,
and urged that every quarrel cease
    the very day he died.

So praise the Lord for Bunyan,
    the sinner turned to saint:
take up the challenge for yourself –
    go forth, and never faint.

☩

May 2000 - Placed fifth in a competition and published in *Rubies in the Darkness, No.16, 2010*. Permission to reproduce applied for. John Bunyan wrote *The Pilgrim's Progress* while in Bedford Gaol.

ABRAHAM: AN IFFY KIND OF FAITH

Lord, you promised, but
I am a practical person,
I cannot see the means.
I need to know the technicalities –
who, what, where, when?
You haven't told me that.

Yes, Lord, I see your meaning, but ...
it simply isn't possible.
We are alone, the two of us
and one faithful servant
who is everything, but nothing –
all I have of flesh and blood, not mine.

And yes, of course I'm capable of counting, but ...
stars and sand are gritty bits of nature,
one so distant, the other rough beneath my feet,
uncountable, impossible –
you try me to extremes,
Yes, I believe in you, Lord, but ...

I see the sun declining, night must come.
The birds have gone to roost,
now I and this abhorrent sacrifice remain.
And I see smoke and haze, and hear a voice
and see the flaming torch of God
which speaks His promise, but ...
can I believe these things of distant history to come?

It seems I must – and yet
some part of me is really doubting still –
I have an iffy kind of faith.

2003 – based on Genesis 15:1-21

MOSES

You didn't give God an easy time of it.
He called,
you stalled.
You made excuses, pleaded weakness,
said you were inarticulate,
too young at forty,
tried everything to get out of a job.

You didn't give Aaron an easy time of it.
He came.
Your shame
was making him, your brother, almost like a slave;
first as your interpreter,
then your scapegoat,
trying everything to make him take the rap.

You didn't give Miriam a happy time of it.
She sang.
You rang
the changes time after time, treated her cruelly.
She was a woman, servant, not a sister,
her humanity nothing to you.
You wouldn't remember her part in your success.

You had given Pharaoh a hard time of it too.
He ruled.
You fooled
him into thinking he could gain the upper hand,
then led him to disaster.
He lost an army.
Your bitter-sweet victory walled you in fear.

You don't give history an easy time of it now.
All laws
were yours,
fashioned to exert a discipline
far beyond reasonable human capacity.
There is no comfort
in a legalistic strait-jacket of rules and regulations.

And now, are you giving the angels an easy time of it?
Who plans
each man's
final destiny now you don't direct the pulse
but have had to clamber down from sight of Promised Land –
prophet, priest and law-maker no more?
Is heaven really big enough to hold you now?

1998

NO WAITING

There was no waiting,
    only pain to be endured no more.
You saw a corridor of opportunity
    that time forgot to mark
and crept away, without goodbyes.

There was no waiting –
your present stays unopened:

You left no forwarding address.

July 2004 – At Bristol Coach Station, en route for home the day following my father's unexpected death.

I AM THE MAN

I am the man –
the man whom Jesus healed,
face to face in darkness,
then his touch, unpleasantly,
the healing pool –
and light – radiant light.
But then I saw him, face to face
and read both love and pain –
because of me.

I am the man –
the self-same man you saw once sitting here
begging for your help,
knowing you walked on
because you knew I couldn't see!
But I could hear –
lack of sight heightens hearing power –
You didn't know -
nor could your sighted eyes
read pain in mine.

Yes, I am the man
and now I'll show you what I am,
increase my strength
work for my keep,
in debt to no one but
the one who healed me,
shared my pain
and understood my need –
the One whose name is Love.

2017 – Based on John 9:7

Places ...

JOURNEY'S END

Silvery sand,
    Soft Sand
And the wind in your face,
    A still wind;
A cloud in the sky:
    A black cloud,
At the end of the road.

The journey takes you from Carlyon Bay
    On the coastal way,
By the golf course
    Where the rich folk play.
But you are poor:
    Keep to the path,
The bracken,
    The gorse.

Follow the line of the railway track
    As it winds and bends
    Along the beach.
Forth and back
    To Polgrever Bay.
But you are clothed,
    An object of fun:
    Keep on your way.*

Barren rocks,
    Mossy and black;
The bare stones of a sandless cove
Where the waters break,
    Green to your eyes,

On the Spite Beach,
    A view of Polkerries
    And a concrete world.

Bright to your eyes,
    Creamy white –
The giant complex
    Of china clay.
The path is diverted,
    Encaged in wire,
And leads to reality.

And you follow the road,
    A winding road,
Which leads to Par
With its layers of streets,
    White and bright,
And the path to the beach –
Your journey's end.

Capture it all
    In a photograph:
Cars and caravans,
    Tents and trailers,
Children, toys and the family dogs,
    And painted beach huts
    From a newly grey seat
As the rain spatters down,
    Beating retreat.

July 1982 - Carlyon Bay, Cornwall.
* Polgrevor had a reputation as a nudist beach!

WISH YOU WERE HERE!

Under an overcast sky,
in the shadow of Big Ben,
I wrote shiveringly ...

> *Having a wonderful time in the Big City –*
> *weather fine,*
> *scenery fantastic –*
> *company great.*
> *Wish you were here.*

Addressed, stamped, despatched,
I left it there in the City
to begin its long journey ...

and turned, alone,
to face the impartial crowd,
oblivious of my existence.
They didn't care
whether I stayed or not,
had no regard for company I didn't keep.

I walked the Square,
the monuments looked down
unsmilingly:
they also didn't care.
    I longed for home –
        and company.

Wish you were here!

September 1994 - Postcard from Westminster - Part of a Trilogy.

WATCHING PEOPLE WATCHING PEOPLE WATCHING THE GRAND CANYON
at The Royal Academy

Backs and bottoms,
handbags, platforms, sandalled feet, screwed shirt backs,
children marshalled to sit down, shut up,
ensconced in ancient leathered armchairs,
keep silence uncomfortably,
aware of eyes, disdained annoyance.
It cannot last.

Eyes tired with watching,
the real view obscured by bodies
aching back buffeted by schoolboys
resting and not looking:
the serious minded tuned-in to their guidebooks,
shutting out the noise,
the know-all teachers who know nothing
imparting great unwitnessed secrets of its manufacture.

Passing opinion on the vast arrangement,
sixty canvases apiece, garish colours oozing
unreality. Remarks ignorant, insulting,
uninformed.

A peace begins unfolding.
The schools march on and leave the connoisseurs
to gaze in undiminished wonder
at achievements they can only dream of.

Meanwhile, a dozen images of Kew have brought to mind
the Real Thing ...

July 1999 - *The Grand Canyon* by David Hockney.

THE VILLAGE

Neat and clean – and empty.

It was not always so.

Once, where flower-strewn 'Bakehouse Cottage' stands,
and Bakehouse now with ivy-cushioned walls,
a thriving industry produced our daily bread,
hot and pungent, lined on iron trays:
wholesome food, good to touch and smell - and taste.
Variations on a piece of dough, rolled, twisted, cajoled into shape;
rock buns, fruit cake, something less exotic for the poor.
Gingermen to mark some special treat or great reward.
And every special day of days – birth, baptism, and lovers tying knots
with rings or marriage lines,
and all the anniversaries kept –
a hand-made cake, so carefully endowed,
would decorate the celebration board.

And once, into the 'Blacksmith's Yard',
would ride the farmers, leading shires
or sportsmen getting ready for the hunt
and wagoners with hardy steeds to shoe;
then every beast would trust the blacksmith's steady hand
and feel the pride with which he served their needs
to guarantee their comfort on the way.
The women took their knives, the men their swords,
to seek a sharper, keener blade for all their chores
and cleaner action in the fields or wars.
He was a man, the blacksmith,
big and tough, and grimed with heat,
but he was held respected for his trade.

So too the wheelwright plied his skills
where now the only reference
resides in 'Wheelwright's Cottage' and the sign
that tells of craftsman's learning, noble art,
Precision tools, a careful eye
for lives were in his hands –
the wagon wheels, the farmer's cart,
the carriages for lord and maid,
the children's treat, the funeral bier –
all fashioned for their task and made
of seasoned timber, deftly turned,
finished and primed for all events,
to go through flood and mud and storm.
It was his livelihood, he could not fail
to offer service of the finest grade.

There was a time when learning took prime place.
The segregated schools have left their trace –
the doors marked 'Girls and Infants',
'Boys' another side,
to mark an education incomplete,
yet worthy of the eagerness they sought
by those who had their passport pence in hand
and plumbed the universe, all learnt by rote,
superior to the poor, who still were taught
the rudiments of math and A-B-C,
through generous benefaction of the 'town',
by teacher resident in her own cott.
But much responsibility resided in one house,
palatial dwelling-place of he who taught
and often was a tyrant, short of grace.

And did the Parson in his 'Close'
once offer cure for souls of deepest kind
or simply empty penitential task
or moral strictures and an early doom?
He may have cared as shepherd for his flock,
or Judas-like, preferred the coffers filled
by worshippers at daily office, weekly tryst,
most going home as burdened as they came.

The church still stands, its doors fast-closed to casual call,
indictment of its failure with the few
who find no place in Sunday pew
and no respect for others' right of entry undefiled.
Once many weekly flocked to hear the Word –
The church stands witness to that time, long demised,
when God was given honour in His world.

From one end of the High Street to the last
the marks of one-time busyness are few -
no trade, no barter, nothing changes hands.
Only village public house still stands,
survivor of commercial holocaust –
of little count in life's necessities,
a blot upon the scene, veiled to disturb
the tranquil mood of death upon this place.
For every other trade or industry,
servants to body, soul and mind,
have passed away and left their empty shells,
flower-bedecked, a resting-place at night
for weary labourers in the city race
who have not time to stop, yet need their space.

And where folk met to read and re-create
their leisure time well-earned till ages great,
only a plaque remains between two cotts
to tell the world that once this was its spot,
and where all life in focus lay,
garden parties, fetes and fine array.
The Lord and Lady gone, a country-club
usurps last vestiges of former pride;
and once a tidy chapel, tucked away,
proclaimed the Gospel of another day,
and loud harmonium accompanied
strange sounds that followed from its cue.
Now neater still, designer-décor sports,
with dulled distinctive windows left in view
and nothing there to indicate the hue –
no book, no date-mark, plaque or tomb...

And while we focus on the dead
who lived, and when they died
withdrew the breath of commerce from this place,
so sad, that even in such pallid awe
the dead fall victims to the vandals' glee.
So what remains? The fields are still as green
but littered with a skyline not their own,
and ploughed and sown by mechanistic art
that squeezes out the past with every grain
and leaves the effluent to start that work again –

Neat, clean and tidy? Yes, and dead!

June 1994 – A Cambridgeshire village visited while on a church weekend – with a bus stop at the World's End!

DIVINE EXPERIMENT

Air
ether
sea and sky
elemental
components of a universe well-made
creation of the Lord of Grand Design
experiment
in cosmic
order
good.

2004 – Tetrachtys

Sixty - 40

DAMP IN DEVON

Morning mists
dispersed late
leaving bright hope
shot with promise
of a better day.
Air, heavy,
reflected the atmosphere,
damp in Devon.

Then the rain
falling leaden
on unyielding flags,
ricochets from tiles
to tarmac, unremitting,
soaking grass, shrubs,
seeping into undergrowth:
welcome home!

Rain-washed roofs
glinting in sunlight,
air fresh,
clouds vying for access –
blue sky lighting the distance.
Brighter vision
portending hope:
England.

★

November 1998

COMING BACK TO ST. OLAVE'S

I had not thought to be back so soon,
back to the silence behind the traffic roar,
enfolded by cool walls out of the hot sun,
a place to rest my weary feet,
bare my soul
and forget time.

Here I conjure with memories of moments past:
the rose at the altar reminiscent of wedding spray,
tangerine and white – bridesmaid, bride,
colour matched.
She had roses in her hair.
Thirty years ago, another time, another place:
but now, just in this moment, I am here,
remembering.

Here I found healing – through touch, prayer, at gifted hands;
here has been peace when all outside screamed war.
Now I come thanking, remembering the pain,
yet thankful still
my House of Healing waits with open doors.
I may look up, be grateful
and be gone.

August 1995 - St. Olave's Church, Exeter, following our move from Cullompton to Dunkeswell. St. Olave's was one of six mediaeval churches in Exeter City Centre.

SOFT SHOES

Lines from a Hospital Ward

Night.

The ward is steeped in silence.
Sleepless patients lie in pain
feeling forgotten,
longing for the welcome sound
of soft shoes on the subdued floor.

*Will they be heading their way
or someone else's?*

Any shoes will do
but the best will bring a brief relief,
some comfort or encouragement
and, most of all,
a date for going home!

February 2011

SPECIFICATION

Mankind is no more.
Humankind is one, is all –
Gender specific.

February 2004

WALES IS ANOTHER COUNTRY

Mist-covered mountains sweep silently towards the green valleys.
In the hillside the grey slate protrudes,
breaking out from the bracken and gorse
and the flowers struggling for life,
adding their pink and purple to the stark greyness.
Foxgloves proliferate by the wayside,
and on every hill, behind every hedgerow
the white dots of hundreds of shorn sheep –
sheep invading every corner, on the roads, in the ditches,
danger zones: running from trains, hastening to traffic,
following the grassland trail
till it reaches those insurmountable slate slopes,
their playground of best Welsh slate –
for Wales is another country.

As rain falls, and gales blow,
sunshine bursts through black clouds,
fails to dry the trenches of mud underfoot
in the paths through woodlands,
filled with birdsong and nature's noise,
of rushing waterfalls, gurgling streams
where trees drip diamond drops of rain;
in the distance the bleating of lost lambs.

Down to beaches, estuaries where brush meets sand
and harbours embrace the waters spreading out to sea.
Golden sand, rough sand, grey sand, shale and pebbles,
all take their places along the varied coastline.
Here are no sheep, only the cries of gulls
and the squabbling of jackdaws vying for space
as they swoop on roofs and gardens seeking sustenance.
No gulls or jackdaws roam the slate cliffs:
they are sacrosanct, the best Welsh slate of a bygone age
alive today on the hillsides.

For Wales is another country
where hikers and seasoned walkers ply their trade
regardless of weather and rough terrain,
lured by the challenge
and the mist-clad mountains.
Like sheep they wander, dotting the scene
as the sheep run and stumble out of their way,
to heights remorseless grey swathes of slate,
best Welsh slate ...
for Wales is another country.

Tywyn, July 2012

DESIRE

O that I could find a place

unspoilt by technicalities and greed –

a corner of a garden where God's Grace

pours Spirit pow'r through every planted seed:

a paradise of bird-song; perfect peace.

August 2002

POETRY AND PRAYER

✝✝✝✝✝✝✝✝✝✝

OLD POEMS

Sheaves of paper,
titled, dated,
records of my poetry, my life.
even without the words
I feel the pain of times, events
that brought their birth,
the hurting and the partings
fashioned each
on questioning foundation:
where, what and would,
why, how and when
and all the time I knew
the answers in the fear
that brings them tumbling back today
while I had thought the writing of the words
had been enough
to shake them from my memory
for ever.
I was wrong.

September 2001

JUST A CHIP

It wasn't a trip
but a slip
on a chip –
a potato chip
not a microchip –
and I damaged my hip.
What a quip
on a slip!
Just a blip?
Did I flip
at the slip?
An embarrassing slip
on a chip:
not a cut on the lip,
but a bruise on the hip,
not a hop or a skip
but a slip
on a chip.

What a drip
took a dip
and pulled out a chip,
then lost his grip
while taking a sip -
or was it a kip
or a nip
or the pip,
or a rip
in the paper, a tip
of the packet, the chip
on a trip
so my usual zip
took a slip
on that chip
dislodging my hip -
not an ego trip
but a slip

of the chip.

May 1999 – based on an incident in a Honiton precinct!

SUN, SEA, SAND

Sun, sea, sand: illusions.
Poets are elusive,
art becomes recluse,
purveyor of beauty,
trapped behind an ugly run-down edifice.

Sea, sand, sun: delusions.
What quirk of creativity
creeps away behind locked doors,
camouflaged in studio-cum-garage?

Sand, sea, sun: allusions.
Make connection in the heat
and watch a friendship cool,
communications cut mysteriously,
unreasoned, buried in a Dorset wilderness.

August 2004

COMPETITION

Who wins the prize?
The man (or woman) likely to surprise
or compromise,
shock into submission,
begin a sentence 'and ...'
and follow on, graffiti-like,
with words that violate
and desecrate
the language
of the bard.

Who holds the key
to victory
in forms of creativity?
The one who sacrifices
art for accolades,
dissects the papers,
rakes the drains
or hacks the Yellow Pages?

Once it was she (or he)
who ate up every diction'ry,
raided encyclopaedias
and studied every variant form
for mastery of the muse.
But now, it seems,
the stuff of dreams
is fashioned to confuse –
nor can this phallic imagery
face likelihood to lose.

It is a travesty of birth,
of form and matter,
substance and content
that such disordered ramblings
should find a precedent
in all unholy vices
and what the cat dragged in.

If I could only plunder
adjudicating minds,
and prisms rend asunder
and probe the electronics,
pick out the recipe,
perhaps I'd be successful
and reap a prize or two –
but would I find fulfilment?
I haven't got a clue!

April 1997

PAGES IN GOD'S STORY

Lord God, we are pages in Your story,
each one an opportunity
to show the way You transform lives,
turning sorrow to joy,
despair to hope,
death to life.

May each of our pages
be a witness to Your Love and Power in the world
today
and always.

August 2010 – based on Psalm 30

Sixty - 50

THE BALLAD OF A 'LOST' SHEEP

I am the 'lost' sheep – but only in others' eyes.
As I wander through the digital wood
I choose my own way,
I have the gifts and abilities, knowledge and intuition:
I choose how I use them or not use them.
If I wish to stay in a world of mail snails
where I am happy and fulfilled,
why should I veer from my path?
I may leave my 'comfort zone' whenever I wish
but I choose to stay,
even when options are being whittled away.
I will not be coerced
into spaces I have no desire to inhabit.

I am the sore thumb on the digital keypad –
I resist its desire to pull me into its cold screen,
preferring print on pretty paper.
I make my own choices.
My technology may be ready and raring to go –
I remain unconnected.

January 2014

SUMMER HAIKU

Summer came early –

Brief span, but in its wake

rain bled carelessly.

June 2007

WITHOUT THE BLUEPRINT

You've given me a gift, dear God ...
that's fine.
People have said, "How wonderful!"
They've recognised the gift,
applauded, welcomed it –
but never for themselves.
I have offered its fruit freely –
they just don't want to know,
which leaves me questioning:

This gift you've given to me,
yes, it helps me through my hurts,
but is that all it's meant to be?
Is it a fact that any hope of sharing
really is a fantasy
of self-projection, as I'm told?
Then what good is it?

Why did you bother to gift me in the first place
without the Maker's blueprint
to tell me what it's FOR?

May 1998

MULTIPLICATION TABLE

God created two
two became two million
ad infinitum

February 2004

A MODERN MASTERPIECE

What makes a masterpiece?
Pencil lines haphazardly drawn
miraculously become an image –
dove of peace
or 'portrait of my cat.'
Childish figures bent on adult deeds,
suggestion over-ruling fact.
Or colourful abstracts, carefully composed –
a myriad boxes,
paper flowers, or concertina'd reading books.
And what of sickly splodges, random thrown
and hailed as innovation by the few
with cast-iron stomachs and averted eyes?
Reality looms large in rusting ships,
derelict dwellings,
litter-ridden fields
and bottle-shattered streets.

Where now are seascapes, tree-lined fields
sheep-filled hills
and flora in abundance?
A long-lost pastoral idyll?
Or buried with the knights beneath
a supermarket car park?

July 2013

SILENT PAINTING

Colour on canvas
stark indigo vies with
playful saxe,
lines of purity besmirched
contrast the hidden depths
of crimson blood revealed
and sunkist orange ocre sea –
each brush stroke
speaking volumes
feelingly.

July 1999

PROMISE

Slithers of colour, arching

without beginning,

tracing rainbows in the rain.

June 2001

THE ONLY DECENT MIRACLE

The Wedding at Cana

The only decent miracle?
The one that's sent a million to their death,
a million million ruined lives,
a billion misread messages,
a trillion petty crimes, unwanted pregnancies
and broken homes.

The greatest miracle of all
would be to turn the wine to water,
redirect the Spirit's course
and start again.

July 1999 – based on Christopher Orr's painting. *The Only Decent Miracle* at the Royal Academy Summer Exhibition.

MUSIC OF LIFE

Music of life, the sound soars:

aims long buried, thoughts long past

reach a crescendo in my heart.

May 1996

A CENTURY OF SONG

We've passed the age of Wesley,
    of Watts and Sankey, too:
the present generation
    just hasn't got a clue
that such momentous music
    could fill the heart with praise
and raise it up to heaven
    until its closing days.

We once sang 'Rule Britannia'
    as Victoria ruled the waves
and sent her troops to battles
    and often to their graves.
The First War they sang ditties
    to keep the boys aglow;
they then packed up their troubles –
    sure God had made it so.

The Second found them crooning
    romantic ballads all,
which still bring tears to many eyes
    that saw their loved-ones fall.
And in among the bullets
    they jived into the night
using up the energy
    they should have kept to fight.

The 'fifties brought the Comets
    that fell at five o'clock
to brighten up the Shadows
    and make the nation rock.
The 'sixties hailed the Beatles,
    their records on release.
Then John and Yoko went to bed
    to call the world to peace.

When Andrew and his brother
    first strung their instruments,
one stole the shows of London –
    while the cello played events.
And now we have Cliff Richard,
    that grand old man of pop,
who sang to the Millennium
    and made it to the top.

The words were old, but they were new
    to modern girls and boys
who'd thrown out faith in Jesus
    with all their worn-out toys.
So now we come with singing
    to mend our hopes and dreams,
and Kendrick, Field and Fred Pratt Green
    are turning up the seams.

May 2000

GOD'S MUSIC

God on the journey,
Lord of the sea,
play me Your music
as history.

November 2005

GOD OF ALL GIFTS

God of all gifts,
we thank you for the gift of words,
words on paper,
words flowing from minds and hearts,
words read, heard, felt, assimilated,
words to describe beauty
    but also the reality of ugliness;
words to bring comfort and hope,
    but also truth and reality;
and most of all we thank you for the One
    Who is the Word,
Who is the greatest of all gifts,
Your Son, our Lord and Saviour,
to whom we dedicate the fruit of all our words.

November 1998 – based on 1 Corinthians 12:4-11

JUST A PERFECT NUMBER

Just thirty lines of poetry to put a world to right
when thirty thousand summers have failed to win the fight!

Yet it took just thirty seconds at the time the rot first set
and thirty decades later we haven't solved it yet.

So will it take just thirty words to demonstrate the fruit
of human inhumanity with greed in stem and root?

We need a social order that's fair and just and right,
with no one homeless on the streets or other desperate plight.

There must be work for all to do, we have to learn to share.
There'd be no poverty in sight if people tried to care.

But politicians can't succeed in bringing this about,
not thirty words, nor thirty lines, but one black concept **out** –

The force that beggars and derides, that eats into the soul
of all that's just and good and true, and stops it being whole.

That word, the darkest one of all, leaves all good standing still:
Thirty silver pieces once spelt out its evil will,

while God's own Prince of Peace had thirty years and three
to bring about a change of heart before eternity.

So how expect mere humans, whatever shade or hue,
to weave the kind of miracle that only God can do?

'Be Red, not dead!' the clarion call came thirty years ago –
now Red is dead, but evil deeds continue – that we know.

A rose by any other name, blood-red and smelling sweet
will wilt in heat of argument, whoever sees defeat –

and Cambridge or delphinium blue, or yellow as the sun,
or green as grass, or hybrid, all parties show as one

when faced with falling polls threat'ning their livelihood.
It's easy to be biased, talk of peace and brotherhood

when sitting on the sidelines not battling at the front –
but for each day's trading figures it's the poor who bear the brunt.

February 1995

DON'T SWITCH OFF!

    Lord, you are merciful,
    full of grace and truth;
    please hear our prayer
    and take notice of us.
    Don't switch off your divine hearing aids
    but turn up the volume
    so we can reach you.

September 2024

DEFINING LOVE

Love
is more than instinct matching chemistry, throbbing
pulses, eyes aglow
meeting over coffee cups, daintily
lifted from white saucers
to vie with lips magnetising nearer,
merging, closing, letting go
to meet again.

Love
is more than feelings, empty, full,
a yearning hollowness, a gut
reaction, charted waters set to lull
the unsuspecting out of sense or time;
more than ethereal realms, sublime
locations, signals to a heartbeat, and
oblivious to pain.

Love
is the pain, pain of loneliness,
of birth and rebirth fashioning each spring,
of life, of death, of seething bitterness,
lost opportunities to demonstrate
diversity, its powers to create
new forms, and to destroy for sport the living thing:
this aching heart.

Love
is the joy of knowing all things new,
of bud and flower, birds on wing,
of colour, taste, perfume in every hue,
moments of otherness, created form –
the shrivelled body pleading to be warm,
the broken spirit, tears becoming
object of love's art.

Love
is a force, a sacrificial fact
that draws humanity into its thrall,
as players on life's stage: the final act,
one all-embracing encore, fashioned fit
to burst its seams, proclaiming, "This is it!"
For love is life, yet life is never all
except to be engulfed in the Divine.

Love
is sacrifice, giving till it hurts,
is life, is death, undying memory,
a void so full, yet squeezed of all deserts,
selfless, unseen, unheard, a silent sense
of wonderment, self-giving, free, yet tense,
embraced, encompassing – humanity
enmeshed in the Divine.

August 1998

SHEPHERDING

What sightless devotion!
Not anymore looking at the grazing which misled
    them
but firm into the shepherd's eyes,
gazes of adoration, longing
to take me home, my friend.
I'll trust you with my life.
Alone I stray, I follow paths that lead to thickets,
catch me in brambles, leave me nettle-stung
and far from home, security and mother-love.

March 2000

RAISED TO HEIGHTS SUBLIME

They did not understand you, Lord,
as you told your friends about a time
when you would not be with them,
but raised to heights sublime.

They had no inner hearing
to interpret myth from fact,
no way of comprehending
the mystery you'd enact.

Before their eyes, then out of heaven
they saw the cloud which veiled the light.
And you, who briefly had sojourned,
seemed to have vanished from their sight.

And still they had no words to show
that miracle they'd shared a part,
they faintly heard, they dimly saw
that you resided at the heart.

Of all they did and all they were,
enabling them to take the rein
and preach with confidence the news
that one day you would come again.

And so you will, Lord, but meanwhile
we see your glory passing fair
and through the cloud, beyond the light
we know and feel you everywhere.

May 1996 – based on John 7:33-34 and Acts 1:9-11

Sixty

MINISTRY AND MISSION

My last official service as a Methodist Local Preacher took place at Hasland Methodist Church on Christmas Day 2024. The theme was 'Gifts' and instead of a sermon I used a story and poetry previously written, including one reflection, written in May 2011, that looked back at Joseph's response to the events leading up to Jesus' birth.

THE ARRIVAL

I remember that journey (how could I forget?),
a few hours' travelling that felt like a week,
with a burden that grew in my heart every mile,
spurring me on yet sapping my strength.
I knew in my bones there was no time for pause
and I prayed that our faithful old beast would survive.
He never complained, didn't even refuse
as the weight on his back became more intense.
She said very little, tried so hard to be brave
but the pain on her face revealed all
and the unspoken question on all of our lips:
'How long before we arrive?'

I was near to collapse when the lights came in view,
so welcome, their shadows gave me no clue
that relief might be short and joy unfulfilled.
The world was awash with visions and noise,
the braying of donkeys and birds in their flight,
and parents calling their children to heel.
But the signs shrieked 'full house' wherever I looked
For we'd left it too late in all kinds of ways -
while the soft-spoken question now burned on my brain:
'Have we arrived?'

As I looked at my loved one I knew without doubt
and a dark despair clutched me deep down inside
that I'd failed both wife and her unborn child
plus the beast who had carried them so far that day.
And what of the God who had given me His trust?
I remember now, with shame in my heart
how my mind had run off to question my lot -
the how, when and where of the task I'd been given,
and the way it was ending before it began.
I railed at Him voicelessly, wits almost gone
as I clung to the bell of the very last hope.

The innkeeper came with the same old response
then looked beyond to her pleading face
and the beast almost gasping his last.
As the darkness descended her prayer had been heard:
I came to in a stable and turned round to find
that the Son who'd been promised had safely arrived.

★

THIS ONE MOMENT

Our lives of service are but preparation
for this one moment out of time,
'twixt our unseeing darkness
and the radiance of His Light.

To those who have walked with Him
He now holds up the lamp,
and those left still to follow
are not lost to His sight.

April 1990

SPEAKING HIS NAME

I cannot help but shout His Name abroad –
He saved me, loves me, walks on by my side.
I cannot help but share the things He's done –
and what He is, and how He will abide
here in my heart
the live-long day.

I cannot still the torrent of my words,
maintain a secret silence or pretend He isn't here.
I cannot but speak out and say, "I know
because He's given me His Name and that is dear:
I treasure it. He made it mine,
so now I am His child.

I can't withhold a day that is His due.
I can't deny Him room, usurp His space.
This is His hour to share, set by, though still
the world is rushing by at such a pace
and doesn't hear Him name His Name –
Redeemer for us all.

November 1999

AN ALTERNATIVE CREED

I believe in God,
not in some celestial architect
weighing me in the balances
and finding there some want;
not in some great benevolence
beaming down and rewarding points for goodness,
or princely potentate
who needs to be obeyed.

God is Spirit,
and when I worship Him
I am engulfed in Him
and He is all to me –
Parent Power, strength and sustenance
Who gives me, not at whim, but need.
One I can trust,
on Whom I can rely.

And I believe in Jesus,
incarnation of Sonship,
very Man upon the earth
and yet the essence of Divinity.
He shows me God
in loving acts, compassion, need.
He gave himself in service,
met each need and bore all wrongs:
the scapegoat, substitute, and great example
all in one,
blood innocent, yet victim of all greed,
gentle giant, ravaged lamb,
He meets all creeds,
makes holy what is dirt
and hauls me from the pit of my desire.

I believe in Spirit,
not the flitting spectre from the tomb
or demons that inhabit human mind
and show themselves in horror themes,
but that Great Force of holiness
that falls at will like fire on my head,
the inexpressible made known,
seen and felt, if never understood;
the Power that says *I am your God,
I come to you, I live in you,
work through your hands, your voice, your touch,
to heal and comfort, power and support.
I am in you, as you are found in Me;
one unit for the showing of My Grace.*

Yes, I believe in God,
Father, Son and Spirit, all in One,
three-fold in person, and yet living still
in single sense, each human heart a home,
a working-place,
a house of rest in Him.
If He were so describable
that I could lay my finger on a word
to express the inexpressible,
define what cannot be defined,
I would ascend and steal His place, and then
he would be God no longer,
not One, not Three,
not anything at all –
but neither, too, would I,
for without Him the universe would die.
There is much jargonese can try
and parcel Him in words and theoretic forms,
but there's not language left for me to use
except to say that
I believe.

September 1995

IMPOSSIBLE TASKS

Lord God, You call us to your service,
you give us impossible tasks,
but you give us the words and the means to do them.

Lord God, you call us to obedience,
you give us the tasks and the power,
and whether or not others heed your call, we must obey.

Lord God, you have put us where we are,
you have called us to work here, now,
and you will not accept any excuses, for you are with us.

But the work is not always sweet to the taste
or pleasing to the ear.
Sometimes it is bitter and rejected, but in you we must
    persevere
Grant us the strength and the will, we pray.

♥

November 1999

CREATIVE THERAPY: FACING THE QUESTION – IN SEARCH OF AN ANSWER

It was not meant to be,
    this catalogue of wrongs,
but rational thought escapes me
    if I cannot write it down.

I cannot breach a breaking heart
    if there is no recourse
to written word: it plays a part
    to dull the depth of pain.

I cannot cope with silent tears
    that stream inside my mind,
I need the recollected years
    to bring the floodtide through.

I can't attempt to live each day
    as though there were no past;
each time I close my eyes to pray
    I'm helpless, lost, afraid.

And even words elude me
    when I'm tired and aching too;
words to express an agony
    that's trussed up in my heart.

I turn to God for healing now -
    I need the tears to flow;
but there's a dam built high somehow
    I cannot let them go.

So I will pray and think and write
    while I remain alone,
so bruised, yet carry on the fight
    till one should say, I care…

And if that one has hurt me,
    the cause of my distress,.
and only could be sorry,
    I'd forgive and be at peace.

That day, it seems, passed long ago,
    and so my record stays,
that all my future heirs shall know
    I lived, when hope was dead.

Yet what is hope? I analyse
    within those private leaves;
I cut my ego down to size,
    admit my faith is thin.

I've contemplated death and life,
    I've written through the void,
I'd really hoped that after strife
    would come the Homeward call.

Yet was I ready? My own hand
    wrote on and showed me no –
God called me still to take a stand –
    He'd never let me go.

And so the word flowed on and on,
    and sifted wheat from chaff,
but enmity was far from gone
    and gave me no respite.

And all the bruises gathered there
    became an open sore
and left me naked, cold and bare,
    heart-raw and growing weak.

And here I am, with pen in hand,
one question to address:
God calls, but I can't understand
why human Church says NO

January 1995 – following my fourth and final attempt to candidate for the Methodist ministry.

✝

A RARE THING

I did a rare thing today, Lord:
I said No –
Not to you, though some would say it was,
but to the demands of human institutions
posing as the Church.
Perhaps that isn't really fair,
put like that it sounds harsh and cold
or cynical,
or like a criticism out of tune.
You know that isn't true,
that this time it was needful to say NO
so that the next time I
can then say YES to You.

October 1998

FOR MANY GENERATIONS

Lord, you have been our strength for many generations,
You have brought us through doubt and difficulties,
You have removed barriers, brought peace where there is
    enmity:
For these things we thank you, Lord.

Lord, you have been our inspiration.
You have given us gifts with which to serve you,
hearts to love you, minds to contemplate,
lips with which to proclaim your Word.
For these things we thank you, Lord.

Lord, you have been our guide and guardian.
You have watched over our waking and sleeping.
You have shown your love to us even when we forgot
    you.
You have given us a past purpose and a future hope.
For these things we thank you, Lord.

September 1999 – based on Psalm 108

CONNECT

Views from the pews,
from the pens in the pews,
from the preachers in the pews
and the parsons in the pulpits
looking over the pews
to the faces of the people;
looking up from the pages
of the Book with a Purpose
portraying the Person
and the Passion of Christ
through His Pardoning Love
and its penalty clause;
and the prayers of the faithful
for a sense of place,
and an ending point
which is Peace
in a turbulent world.

♥

November 1998 – Part of a Presentation during the recruitment process to appoint an editor to the new Methodist magazine *Connect*. [I came second in the process.]

THE MODERN BABEL

Faced with the modern Babel,
the voices vying for supremacy in a world seeking for
    meaning,
we pray for discernment.
Grant us to rise above the clamour
and reach out for the Truth;
enable us to hear your voice only,
to identify the false prophets and those who spread alarm
and to lead others to the truth.
And enable us, Lord,
to steer clear of the vultures that gather in the private
    places of our lives
and look to you, for freedom and purpose.

August 1998 – based on Matthew 24:15-28

KNOWING GOD

As a child I needed God as Father,
tender-hearted, looking down,
listening to my pleas.

In youth He came as power –
fire, scorching will to burning desires
tempered by peace.

Now I know my need of Him as loving still,
reassuring arms,
the Father-heart of love
but more than that –
the One who takes me as I am
acceptingly.

November 1999

LISTEN!

Listen!
Listen to the sounds of the trees
crying out in the night
as the fire consumes their life-force,
beauty of cypress, cedar, oak,
all their history –
laying bare the forests
of centuries,
the homes of insect, bird
and every creature seeking shelter.
Listen to their crying, their dying,
mournful sounds filling the air
despairingly
till death's silence falls.

Listen!
Listen now to the cries of shepherds
facing their barren pastureland.
Where will the sheep graze now –
their lives, their livelihoods lost
in hunger's bleating?

Listen!
Even the lions roar their own lament,
lost forests, lost protection,
exposed as predators,
kept at bay.
Listen for the sounds of lamentation:
lost forests are lost life.
Only the silent sound of death stalks the land.

Listen –
and you will hear.

January 2015 – based on Zechariah 11:1-3

DEEP IN THE HEART

I cannot comprehend earth's place within the
    universe
as countless planets circle round the sun.
Deep at its beating heart there lies
some mystery that cannot be undone.

I strain to understand the purpose of this life,
what great Celestial Mind ordaining me.
Deep in His creative heart there lies
the promise of a place eternally.

Inhabiting this minute world of ours
a human seed was sown and given life.
Deep in the pulsing heart of time
it grew to manifest earth's strife.

And at the heart of that same universe
there rose One to become the Son of Man.
He took our rights and wrongs and heartache
deep into his soul and its brief span.

Now we may look and see a clearer view,
how ordered planets wait each probing eye.
Black holes lie at their heart of darkness
but Light will never let them die.

That Light – God, Son and Spirit – One
illuminates our world and others now.
Deep at the heart their Light is Love –
whose light will never ever cease to glow.

March 2018

TOO BUSY TO LISTEN

Listen when God speaks to you in your life today.
[Anne Smith]*

Too busy talking,
    not enough listening.
Too busy waiting,
    not enough watching.
Too busy writing – nothing to read.
Life passes by with uncatchable speed.

Too busy arguing
    not enough pause.
Too busy plotting
    no open doors.
Too busy staring – way into space.
Life moving on at incredible pace.

Too busy searching,
    nothing to find.
Too busy groping
    with eyes partly blind.
Too busy doing, no time to be.
Life passes but so little they see.

Too busy hating,
    no time for love.
Far too much knowledge,
    but nothing to prove.
No time for Jesus, no one to call.
Soon in earth's story there'll be no time at all.

Too busy with theories,
    no time to reflect.
Too much conjecturing
    outside context.
Too busy not living, but no time to die.
No questions answered, left asking why.

Too busy being human,
    the only road trod.
No sense of divinity,
    no thought of God.
So busy thinking of what to do next,
while life rumbles on and leaves us perplexed.

Are we so busy
without giving thought
to the pictures around us,
    the lives all so fraught;
so much distracted God's voice can't be heard
when He wills us to listen, to treasure His Word.

How **can** we be busy
    with our own little care
when out there is a world
    that now sinks in despair,
in a mire of destruction from which it can't climb
until someone listens and gives it more time?

♥

February 2021 - * Sunday Service for 14th February, *The Methodist Recorder,* 7.2.21.

PRAYER SEVENTY-FIVE

But when did such bravado serve your Kingdom, Lord,
sat down and held a hand
or gave an arm
or shed a mutual tear,
then looked toward the days ahead
with hope when all despaired?

Does every last defiance of propriety
give honour to your Name
and every empty accolade
urge one soul nearer Home?
Has this three-quarter century
been use to you at all?

Lord, could I ever once expect
to reach so great an age
to entertain its limitations gracelessly
while skipping over roads without a thought
except to dodge a coming vehicle?
It seems I cannot act my age.

Is it because my mind dictates
I must not lose
the sense of being young
though looks belie the dream?
Or is it just another ego trip
to be indulged with every passing hour?

Forgive me, lord, for failing you so much,
for making my ambitions paramount,
promoting me above your Word of Life
and in this daily dying
not to myself
but to your promises?

Yet Lord, let me, despite the trickling time,
have energy enough to run on in the race
and never lose that impetus to live
and work and see some dream fulfilled –
and most of all, whatever else befall,
be there for those who need me
in **Your** Name.

8th July 2016

REMEMBRANCE

I remember – signs, symbols, sacred presence,
    bread, wine, robed red sacrifice,
      torn flesh, bleeding, nailed hands, lanced side,
      forgiving – all for me.

I remember – bread, wine, communion shared,
    memorial meal, sacred pledge, saving grace,
      living Word, loving Lord,
      dying – in my place.

June 1995

Postscript

TWILIGHT HOPE

Here, in the twilight of our lives,
we look back in wonder
at all we've seen and been
and done together –
and we are thankful for the day.
Now we can only look forward
with hope, and trusting that
the future holds for us
one day that will be diamond bright.

♥

July 2024 – Written for Geoffrey on our 59th wedding anniversary.

ACKNOWLEDGMENTS

First of all, my thanks to members of my family and friends who, once the idea had imposed itself during a morning Quiet Time, encouraged me to pursue the production of another 'special events' collection. I hope you will all find something of interest and enjoyment in the result.

Then, once more, to Patrick Mancini, Oonagh Robinson and colleagues at Moorleys who once again undertook to put the book into print, producing such an attractive result.

Previous Publications

[All Cottage Books or PBP unless otherwise stated]

Messages of Devon [1991]
Occult: The Hidden Dangers [with Margaret Oxenham 1991]
Aspects of the Sermon [1993]
Farewell to Wincolmlee [1994]
Time and The Gospel [1995]
Adhering to the Rules [1995, Areopagus 2000]
Fish-cakes and Fantasy [The Winterton Lecture 1996]
Something to Rhyme About [Ed. with Daphne Ayles, 1996]
Letters to The Editor ... [1997]
A World of Love [1997]
Memo to God [1998]
Still Dancing [1998]

Candles in the Darkness [1998]
In Debt to C. S. Lewis [On the influence of his fiction, 1999]
Candles in Draughty Spaces [chapbook 1999]
Fifty Days [2000]
Meeting Jesus [Ed. 2000]
Happy in Hospital [Ed. with Daphne Ayles, 2000]
Lenten Light [2001]
Penitential Tears [2001]
Constantine – with Care! [As Annette Collins, Fiction 2001]
Daughters of Eve [Feather Books 2001]
Advent Women [2018]

Publications in Print

[All by Moorleys]

Prayers for Worship [1997, reprinted 2020]
More Prayers for Worship [2009]
The Bound Lamb and Other Reflections [2013, reprinted 2020]
Reflections on a Journey [2017]
For Many Occasions [2018]
Advent Women [2018]

Recent Studies

[All in A4 typed format, produced by Pointer Print, Hasland]

Teilhard's Tulip – Facing a Question – Seeking the Answer [2022]

Paul, Marriage and Misogyny [2023]

The Hammer of The Lord – Mark for the 21st Century [2024]

The Church on The Green: Hasland Wesleyan Church 1899-1961 [2024]